Hollywood Portraits

Hollywood Portraits

CLASSIC SCENE STILLS 1929-41

MARK A VIEIRA

Bison Books

First published in the UK in 1988
Bison Books Ltd
Kimbolton House
117A Fulham Road
London SW3 6RL
England

ISBN 0 86124 432 X

Printed in Hong Kong

Reprinted 1991

Page 1: A portrait of Jean Harlow by George Hurrell for George Cukor's **Dinner At Eight**, produced in 1933 at MGM. *Pages 2–3:* Virgil Apger's portrait of a Cedric Gibbons set for Dudley Murphy's **The Night is Young**, produced in 1935 at MGM. *Below:* This production still is from Cecil B DeMille's **The Squaw Man**, produced in 1931 at MGM.

DEDICATION: To my mother, my father, my sister and Patricia Tooke

INTRODUCTION

Welcome to my file cabinet which contains a collection of movie stills which I began buying in 1973, as a graduate student at the University of Southern California. My subsequent career as a photographer has both fed, and been fed by, this collection. It's now large enough to occupy an entire file cabinet, and I feel it's time to share some of it with you.

I've purposely limited the scope of my collection; I'm neither a historian nor an archivist. I enjoy collecting movie stills, especially original prints from the Golden Era of Hollywood—the 1930s. Motion pictures from this era were the first that I ever saw. I encountered them, as did the rest of my Baby Boom contemporaries, on local television stations. Like them, I clamoured to be taken to the neighborhood theater to see **Moby Dick, Bambi** and **The Great Locomotive Chase**. Unlike them, I came to prefer 20 year-old movies encountered on television, the relics that my parents fondly referred to as 'classics': **King Kong, Grand Hotel**, et al.

My fascination with these films led me to the Oakland Public Library, in search of books containing photos from them. When I found these photos (usually in the center sections of movie star biographies like Irving Shulman's apocryphal *Harlow*), I also found a way to extend the magical experience of viewing films, to 're-experience' the films.

It was this habit of re-experiencing that led to my passion for collecting movie stills. At about this same time (the mid- to late 1960s), books began to appear at the library that presented movie stills in a more self-sufficient format than did the usual movie star biographies. Daniel Blum's *Pictorial History of the Talkies*, Richard Griffith and Arthur Mayer's *The Movies*, and John Kobal and Raymond Durgnat's *Garbo*

all presented movie stills not only as representations of films, but as legitimate images, complete in themselves. The stills now stood on their own, apart from the movies they'd been created to sell.

I suddenly realized that looking at these stills was just as exciting as looking at the movie itself, and in some respects, even better. The stills held *still*: the moments of beauty that were fleeting and evanescent on the screen could now be studied at leisure. They could even be enshrined on a wall.

And so my collection began with movie books—scrimped and saved for, then sacrificed to a more personal system of organization: I'd cut out my favorite stills and re-assemble them in a binder according to film and studio. If a book was out of print, I'd photocopy the pictures at the library.

My next realization was that this budding collection was unified by something other than mere chronology. There was something in my pictures that unified them and that also differentiated them from stills taken for current films and TV. That 'something' was unique to the 'talkie' era. I first tried to identify it, then to understand it, and then even to emulate it in eight millimeter student films.

What was it that made these pictures so different? What gave them the subjective quality that I found irresistable? It was the *photography* of these pictures that made them different from anything before or since; specifically, it was the *lighting*.

Each of my stills had a glowing, radiant, almost translucent quality. This quality was entirely due to the lighting style of Hollywood's visual artists—the cinematographers and portrait photographers.

When I moved to Los Angeles to attend USC Cinema School, I discovered a host of memorabilia stores, and a network of dedicated movie still collectors, through whom I could elevate my collection to a new level. It was now possible for me to bypass the movie books and go directly to the source of my fascination: original movie stills. Fifteen years and one file cabinet later, I have become that strange but not unique combination of art collector and movie fan.

I seek out pictures of certain movie stars whom I revere as a 'fan,' and yet I will accept only the finest quality photographic print of this star. More importantly, I seek quality in the photographic concept itself—its lighting and design—because I regard the Hollywood 'cameramen' as stars, too. They had just as much glamour as their legendary subjects.

In sharing my collection with you, I also share the love I have for these artists and their models. They've entertained me and educated me. I hope they'll do the same for you.

Mark A Vieira
7 July 1987

Left: Author Mark Vieira as he assisted George Hurrell in shooting a portrait sitting in July 1976. *(Photo by Judy Friend.)*

Facing page: A 1938 portrait of Norma Shearer by Laszlo Willinger. Willinger's skill and taste created the MGM look of the late Thirties, just as George Hurrell had defined the early Thirties, and Clarence Bull the mid-Thirties.

Pages 8–9: A cut scene from **The Cat and the Fiddle**, produced in 1934 at MGM, which was directed by William K Howard and starred Ramon Novarro and Jeanette MacDonald.

'We are no other than a moving row
Of Magic Shadow-shapes that come and go
   Round with the Sun-illumin'd Lantern held
In Midnight by the Master of the Show. . .'

The Rubaiyat of Omar Khayyam

Hollywood's Golden Era, the 1930s, started with a bang. After more than 25 years of silent movies, Hollywood was being shaken by the noisy arrival of talking pictures, or 'talkies,' as they were called sometimes affectionately, sometimes derisively. By the middle of 1929, though, even the most derisive critics of the new-fangled development had to concede that films with sound were a reality. With cataclysmic swiftness, the established order of an entire industry was shaken, changed and in many cases, destroyed.

Above: Greta Garbo sits with director Clarence Brown on the set of her first talkie, **Anna Christie**. Its March, 1930 release was heralded with the slogan 'Garbo Talks!' She and Charlie Chaplin were the last major stars to make the transition to sound. They were wise in waiting, since the early talkies were aurally primitive and visually static.

Facing page: Clara Bow in a 1929 portrait by Paramount Studios' Eugene Robert Richee. The effervescent 'It' girl was one of the first casualties of the talking picture revolution.

Above: Reginald Denny and Kay Johnson in Cecil B DeMille's **Madam Satan**, produced in 1930 at MGM. DeMille was one of the first sound film directors to give back to the movie camera some of the mobility it had enjoyed in the silent days. Meanwhile, MGM's team of glamour experts continued to supply the gloss that would become the standard at this studio in the 1930s. Hal Rosson was the cameraman, Gilbert Adrian designed the costumes, and Cedric Gibbons designed the sets, assisted by DeMille regular Mitchell Leisen, who would soon be directing films of his own.

Facing page: John Gilbert was also a talkie victim. His voice was neither high-pitched nor squeaky; it simply did not match the image he'd projected in silents. He is seen here in a still from Fred Niblo's **Redemption**, his first talkie, produced in 1930 at MGM. It was put on a shelf for months after its completion because of a bad sneak preview. Gilbert was then rushed through a second talkie, **His Glorious Night**, the premiere of which proved to be anything but glorious. The audience snickered at Gilbert's already dated intonations. Neither **Redemption** nor the string of inferior films that followed did anything to restore his popularity.

Above: Marie Dressler won an Academy Award for her tear-jerking performance in **Min And Bill**, produced in 1930 at MGM—a George Hill production.

Facing page: Gary Cooper as Legionnaire Tom Brown in Josef von Sternberg's **Morocco**, produced in 1930 at Paramount. Cameraman Lee Garmes told me that Gary Cooper challenged Sternberg's autocracy on the set of **Morocco** one day after lunch by yawning long and loud. Sternberg then said: 'The next person who yawns will cause this entire company to be dismissed.'

Gary Cooper repeated his yawn and Sternberg, as usual masking his pleasure, closed the **Morocco** set until the next morning. **Morocco** was such a huge success that this extravagant behavior could be temporarily overlooked by Paramount.

Top: Director, *auteur*, and legend, Josef von Sternberg is here seen in a 1930 portrait by Eugene Robert Richee, who was one of the many artists Sternberg used and taught and later discounted. In fairness to Sternberg, though, it must be said that these artists rarely achieved results equal to those they achieved under his Svengali-like tutelage.

Facing page: Advertised as 'the woman all women want to see,' Marlene Dietrich made her American film debut in **Morocco**, the second of seven films she would make in collaboration with her discoverer, Josef von Sternberg.

Previous page: Dorothy Mackaill, circa 1931, exhibits (among other things) the influence that Marlene Dietrich was already having on films of this period. The Sternberg-Dietrich glamour collaboration influenced styles of dress, courtship, and music, as well as photography. Paramount Studios—and Hollywood—would never be the same.

The star system would now depend on—and include—the skilled craftsmen who were able to effect this kind of transformation. Cinematographers like Lee Garmes and William Daniels, heretofore known for their pictorial sensibilities, were now regarded as wizards for their ability to 'glamorize' an actress.

This glamorization had to be transmitted to the printed page: fan magazines were now the most effective means of luring audiences into theaters. Each fan magazine had a rotogravure section devoted to full-page portraits of the stars. 'Salon' portraits fit this format better than did the 'scene stills' taken on the set after each scene by the production still man. As a result, each movie company installed a full-size portrait gallery. It was there that the on-screen images of each star could be emulated by portrait photographers like Paramount's Otto Dyar and MGM's Clarence Sinclair Bull. Before long, these photographers were not merely emulating; they were evolving an approach of their own, and inventing the 'Hollywood glamour portrait.'

Above: The work of Otto Dyar at Paramount reflected the lighting innovations of Lee Garmes and Josef von Sternberg—especially the use of a strong spot light shooting down on a subject from almost directly above, thereby creating a 'north light' effect. This 1933 portrait of Clara Bow reflects the changes in studio portraiture during this period. (Compare it to Clara's picture on Page 11.) It is also a record of her last portrait sitting, made at Fox Films for Frank Lloyd's **Hoopla**, a racy film which was not successful enough to revive her career.

Facing page: Shot by Don English, this scene still of Marlene Dietrich in Sternberg's **Shanghai Express** reproduces Lee Garme's lighting almost as well as a frame enlargement, in that this is how it appears on the screen.

Facing page: Robert Z Leonard's **Strange Interlude**. Norma Shearer, already the First Lady of MGM, is seated on the couch next to Clark Gable in this still, taken on 22 February 1932.

'Bill Daniels started the picture and then was pulled off it because Garbo was starting the last picture of her contract and had to have him on it,' Lee Garmes told me. 'Norma Shearer didn't like it, but there wasn't much she could do about it, even if she was married to Irving Thalberg. Then I came on the picture, and she came to like me better.'

Above left: By the second week of March, Norma Shearer was realizing how lucky she was to have gotten Lee Garmes after his Oscar for **Shanghai Express** and especially after seeing how much better she looked in the rushes; the 'north light' did wonders for her. She had him reshoot her first scene and then proceeded with the rest of **Strange Interlude**. In this production still, we see Lee Garmes leaning forward to smile at a radiant Norma Shearer and a properly respectful Tad Alexander.

Strange Interlude is the only film on which my two favorite cinematographers worked, albeit consecutively. When watching this film, I enjoy pointing out the differences in their respective styles.

Above right: The stern, elegant figure seated at the camera here is none other than William H Daniels, who by this time (1937) was known as 'Mr Daniels' by his colleagues.

What Lee Garmes and William Daniels shared in common was that they each achieved wealth, fame and power by glamorizing a foreign actress at a crucial point in her career. Garmes helped Josef von Sternberg to define the Dietrich 'face.' Daniels helped Irving Thalberg to create the Garbo 'aura.' The history of cinema would have been decidedly less glamorous if not for the teams of Garmes/Sternberg/Dietrich, and Daniels/Thalberg/Garbo.

Above: I enjoy speculating on the results of collaborations that might have happened but never did. For instance, if Marlene Dietrich had been photographed à la Rembrandt by William Daniels for an imaginary MGM production, she might have looked like this 1935 portrait by Richee.

Facing page: Greta Garbo might have gone through her career looking like this if Lee Garmes had applied his north light to her for some imaginary Paramount picture. This portrait is actually by Clarence Bull, circa 1930.

Above: Universal Pictures wisely avoided the glamour issue, concentrating instead on a speciality that no other studio could surpass. Horror films like **Frankenstein**, which the studio thoughtfully released in time for Christmas 1931, created a sensation by appealing to an appetite that psychologists are still trying to understand. James Whale's free adaptation of the Mary Shelley book boasted Boris Karloff as 'the Monster.' Bela Lugosi had been cast in the part, but artistic disagreements worked to Karloff's advantage. He became a star, despite the handicaps of a wordless role and heavy makeup.

When Boris Karloff returned to the horror factory, he occasioned several more classic films. James Whale guided Karloff through an even more sympathetic portrayal in **The Bride of Frankenstein**.

Facing page: James Whale also worked with Elsa Lanchester to create an unforgettable image of a female creature for the title role.

Page 28–29: Elsa Lanchester and Charles Laughton in a 1935 studio portrait, probably by William Walling. Laughton was starring in **Ruggles of Red Gap**, and his wife was appearing in **Naughty Marietta**, a far cry from her monster role. **Ruggles** was a comedy and **Marietta** was a musical; by the mid-1930s both were flourishing.

Above: Nell O'Day was one of many musical stars, dancers, and singers imported from Broadway to populate Hollywood musicals like John Murray Anderson's **The King of Jazz**, produced in 1930 at Universal.

Facing page: Gloria Stuart was recruited for her beauty, as evidenced by this off-set portrait for Frank Tuttle's **Roman Scandals**, a 1933 Eddie Cantor comedy-musical produced by the Samuel Goldwyn Studios.

Above: Perhaps the most well-known of all comedy classics, Frank Capra's **It Happened One Night**, produced in 1934 at Columbia, won Oscars for him, Clark Gable and Claudette Colbert—establishing the comic proficiency of each, as well as raising Columbia Pictures to a level of respectability.

Facing page: No film made by the Fox Film Corporation before 1934 was ever released to television, so the majority of that studio's output remains tantalizingly unseen—including Walter Lang's 1933 comedy **The Warrior's Husband**. It starred Elissa Landi, here shown with Ernest Truex in a role reversal made more striking by Earl Luick's costumes.

Above: Ginger Rogers played radio star Glory Eden in William Seiter's **Professional Sweetheart** produced in 1933 at RKO, a satire on radio personalities. This portrait was made by Ernest Bachrach, and is significant for its use of geometric blocks—a stylistic mannerism pioneered by Metro's Bull.

Facing page: The 'Blonde Bombshell' Jean Harlow started her MGM contract by playing a gun moll in Charles Brabin's **The Beast of the City.** This character portrait was made by Clarence Bull on 17 November 1931.

I asked Mr Bull if there was a story behind his use of geometric blocks in portraits between 1930 and 1934. He explained that the magazines and newspapers had complained to Metro's publicity department that identical poses were being sent to every editor; they didn't want the same picture that was currently appearing in some other magazine.

Bull solved this problem by introducing the geometric blocks into the portrait settings, and by changing the wooden blocks' arrangements from pose to pose in the course of a 200 shot sitting. As a result, no pose had exactly the same configuration of blocks as any other pose.

A further explanation for the ubiquitous blocks could be a Deco or even Cubist influence, but the best explanation for such conventions is usually that they are just that—conventions.

Clarence Bull's portraits of the early 1930s are characterized by a severity of design and a softness of tone. He is best remembered for his near-mystical studies of Greta Garbo, but I find equally amazing his work in other subjects' sittings from this period.

Facing page: Bull made this portrait of John Barrymore on 31 October 1931, as the leonine prince of the theater was about to experience his last flash of fame.

Above: Less than a year later, John's sister Ethel posed for Bull in her costume for **Rasputin and the Empress**, the Irving Thalberg production which featured all three Barrymores. Ethel's oft-expressed disdain for Hollywood is almost apparent here.

Above: Diana Wynyard also came to MGM for **Rasputin and the Empress**, but stayed for only two more pictures before returning to greater success in Britain.

Facing page: Joan Crawford, suffering a momentary lapse in popularity, modeled an Adrian gown for this 25 November 1932 sitting. Clarence Bull was soft-spoken and partially crippled. He showed sensitivity for his subjects' inner moods that some of his contemporaries missed; his subjects, in turn, opened up to him as to few other photographers.

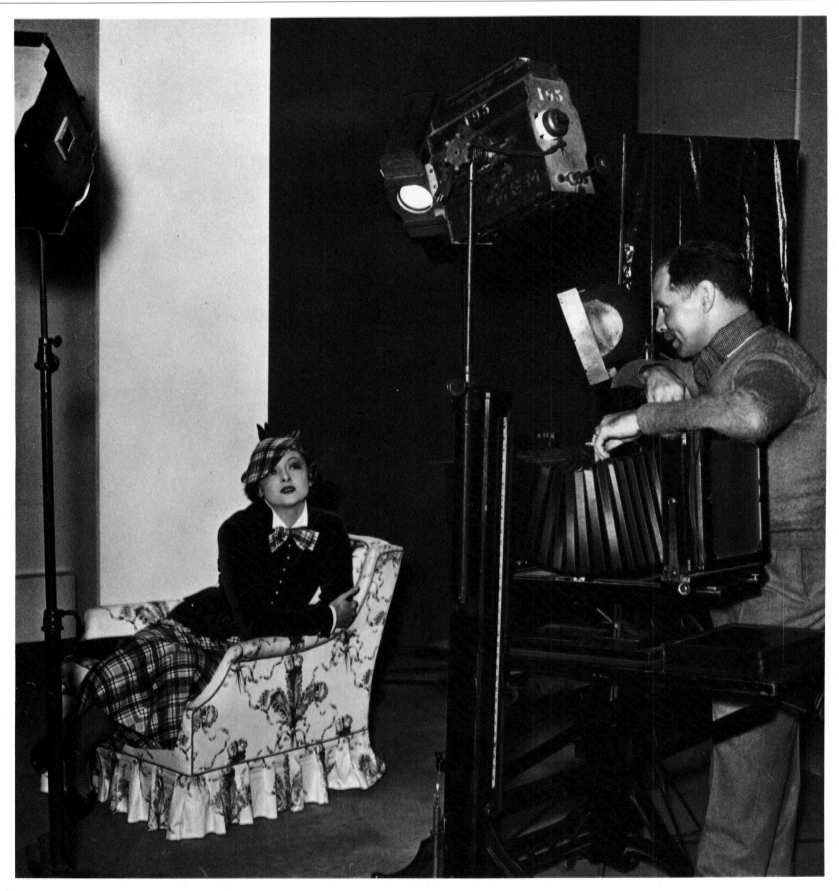

Above: Clarence Bull 'shoots' Myrna Loy in the Metro portrait gallery, which he supervised for more than 30 years.

Facing page: Johnny Weissmuller in civilian garb—as photographed by Bull following the completion of WS Van Dyke's **Tarzan, the Ape Man**, which was produced in 1932 at MGM. Despite the civvies, Weissmuller's roles at the studio were limited to loincloth-and-vine adventures.

Robert Z Leonard's **Susan Lenox: Her Fall and Rise** was a typically exotic 1931 melodrama. It took its heroine, Greta Garbo, through an exhausting sequence of milieus: farm house, architect's lodge, circus sideshow, Manhattan penthouse, and finally a Central American jungle with its port and obligatory cantina, where Garbo was forced to take work as a hootchy-kootch dancer while waiting for long-lost Clark Gable to come down the river.

Above: While Garbo waited for Gable in **Susan Lenox**, Ian Keith wooed her in this private dining room, separated from the cantina by beaded curtains. Alexander Toluboff's imaginatively detailed set has to be seen from two more angles to be fully appreciated.

Facing page: Adrian designed this costume for Garbo to wear in a **Susan Lenox** montage sequence; it appears on the screen for less than a minute.

These pages: This angle shows the entire cantina set from **Susan Lenox**. Garbo and Keith are visible at lower left, under the first microphone boom, waiting for a cue from 'Pop' Leonard. The rows of black flats around the perimeter of the set would appear to give credence to all those stories about Garbo's insistence on privacy.

Pages 46–47: The cantina set as seen from the entrance. Ian Keith is at center, asking proprietress Rose Dione for a private room. Note how cameraman William Daniels uses shadowed areas to create depth.

Above: In this scene from Edgar Ulmer's **The Black Cat**, produced in 1934 at Universal, Bela Lugosi has just pared the skin from Boris Karloff's upper torso in an act of climactic revenge for the murders of his wife and daughter.

Hollywood in the early 1930s was more willing to depict (or suggest) exotic locales, sexual situations, or forbidden practices; the Depression and radio were affecting box-office receipts, and audiences had to be lured back.

Above: After having captive Charles Starrett savagely whipped, Myrna Loy realizes that she has '...conceived a romantic interest in him.' She decides not to kill him, despite the urging of her father, Boris Karloff, in Charles Brabin's **The Mask of Fu Manchu**, produced in 1932 at MGM. Jack Pierce was loaned to Metro with Karloff to make the package complete.

Above: A film that lay unseen for 50 years was Howard Hawks' **Scarface** (1932 United Artists), which starred Paul Muni (shown here) as a despicable character based on Al Capone. Producer Howard Hughes made **Scarface** more violence-ridden than either **Public Enemy** or **Little Caesar**, and by so doing, ensured that it would never be seen on 1950s television. Only after his death were the rights to this celebrated film cleared.

Above: 'It's colossal!' said Frank Reicher as the Captain, upon seeing this set in an earlier scene in **King Kong**, and for once, the adjective was appropriate. Carroll Clark and Al Herman were the film's art directors.

Facing page: An Ernest Bachrach portrait of Bruce Cabot and Fay Wray, who had no idea that **King Kong** would make them immortal.

Above: Can you feature this platinum blonde hair cascading from King Kong's paw? Jean Harlow was RKO's first choice for the role of Ann Darrow in that 1933 film. Only an MGM contract saved this Beauty from that Beast. She is seen here with director Victor Fleming in a publicity shot for **Reckless**, produced in 1935 at MGM, which suggests how she might have looked after a jungle ordeal.

Facing page: Constance Bennett was another popular American blonde, and one who knew the exact bankability of her following. This uncredited portrait is from Gregory LaCava's **Bed Of Roses**, produced in 1933 at RKO.

Above: Carole Lombard, along with Norma Shearer and Marlene Dietrich, took it upon herself to learn the intricacies of photographic lighting technique. By the end of the Thirties, she was as expert as any working cameraman. This uncredited portrait was made for Mitchell Leisen's **Swing High, Swing Low**, produced in 1937 at Paramount.

Facing page: Lombard is primarily remembered as a comedienne who married Clark Gable. In actuality, her 13 year career included roles of every conceivable type. She is shown here in a portrait by Clarence Bull for Jack Conway's **The Gay Bride**, produced in 1934 at MGM.

Above: Gertrude Michael, fresh from singing her *Sweet Marihuana* number, is helped up to a camera platform by the characteristically friendly Earl Carroll.

Facing page: Marion Davies was 36 when this Clarence Bull portrait was made for Raoul Walsh's **Going Hollywood**, produced in 1933 at MGM.

Facing page: Another offbeat musical was Mitchell Leisen's **Murder at The Vanities**, produced in 1934 at Paramount, which introduced *Cocktails For Two*. This backstage scene shows the girls for which Earl Carroll's famous Vanities were so well known. The featured players here are Jack Oakie (in tux), Kitty Carlisle and Carl Brisson.

Above: Carl Brisson and Kitty Carlisle silhouetted against a muslin moon in the *Live and Love Tonight* number from **Murder at The Vanities**, a clever film which deserved to be—and indeed was—rescued from the archives.

Pages 60–61: Paramount's 1934 **Bolero**, unobtrusively directed by Wesley Ruggles, was more a feast for the eyes than an engaging biography of a dancer. Hans Dreier designed the settings, Travis Banton designed gowns for Carole Lombard (here dancing with George Raft) and Leo Tover used dramatic arc lights throughout to make Raft's dance numbers even more effective.

Above: Pictured here are Kathleen Burke, Gary Cooper, Douglas Dumbrille, Franchot Tone and Richard Cromwell—in Henry Hathaway's 1935 classic **The Lives of a Bengal Lancer**. It was intended as an adventure film, yet it was also a tour de force of design (by Hans Dreier) and lighting (by Charles Lang).

Facing page: One Paramount classic badly in need of restoration is Frank Borzage's 1932 **A Farewell To Arms**; it now circulates only in truncated dupe prints. A 1976 screening of a complete print at the Los Angeles County Museum of Art revealed the true greatness of the film. This still shows Gary Cooper and Helen Hayes in one of Hans Dreier's expressionistic sets.

Above: An on-set portrait, probably by Lippman, of Marlene Dietrich in the final scene from **The Song of Songs**. The gown is by Travis Banton and the statue is one of two for which Marlene refused to pose.

Facing page: Marlene Dietrich's first film without Josef von Sternberg was **The Song of Songs**, produced in 1933 at Paramount, which was directed by the equally innovative Rouben Mamoulian. According to Mamoulian, Marlene was not happy away from Sternberg's all-encompassing influence, and tried to bring elements of it onto the **Song of Songs** set. For the first week of filming, Mamoulian was forced to issue a daily request that Marlene restore the angle of her wildly arched eyebrows to the angle where they'd been at the end of the previous day's work; she was after all, playing an innocent country girl, not Shanghai Lily. This portrait was made by still man Irving Lippman outside Marlene's dressing room—in unfiltered sunlight, which was a far cry from the type of still lighting provided for her on Sternberg's sets.

Chinese-American actress Anna May Wong posed for virtually every important photographer of this period, and each man saw a different facet of her unique glamour. Otto Dyar photographed her in costume for Sternberg's **Shanghai Express** *(above)*, a high-key treatment that did nothing to diminish her charm.

Facing page: Here is Anna May Wong in 1937 as photographed by William Walling, who chose to give her a 'low-key' treatment so stark that almost nothing but her bone structure is left. Not even Marlene Dietrich could survive such a steep and dramatic placement of a key light.

Above: Rouben Mamoulian's cinematic imagination found new challenges in the screen's first three-color Technicolor feature, **Becky Sharp**, produced in 1935 at RKO, which starred Miriam Hopkins and was photographed in subtle hues not seen before or since. Ray Rennahan (on stool) was the master colorist.

Facing page: The most famous song-and-dance team in screen history is shown here in a scene still from Mark Sandrich's **The Gay Divorcée**. It was photographed by David Abel, who supplied the creamy visual texture for most of the Fred Astaire-Ginger Rogers pictures.

Above: The headline-conscious Warner Brothers studio was the home of social dramas, gangster sagas and historical epics. Raoul Walsh's 1939 **The Roaring Twenties** starred James Cagney, here seen with Gladys George. She has just sung *A Shanty In Old Shantytown* to the inebriated 'Eddie Bartlett,' a former bootleg baron now reduced to driving taxicabs.

Facing page: Frederick March suffered moral degeneration in Mervyn LeRoy's **Anthony Adverse**, produced in 1936 at Warner Brothers. This expertly made scene still was the work of Bert Longworth.

Above: Olivia DeHavilland and Errol Flynn co-starred for the third of seven films together in Michael Curtiz's **The Adventures Of Robin Hood**, produced in 1938 at Warner Brothers. This still is an example of an on-set portrait posed especially for 'poster art' by the production still man.

Facing page: Mexican actess Dolores Del Rio, who by this point in her decorative career had impersonated every nationality from Brazilian to Polynesian, essayed the role of the celebrated French courtesan in William Dieterle's **Madame Dubarry**, produced in 1934 at Warner Brothers, while wearing a stunning wardrobe designed by Orry-Kelly.

Above: The brothers Warner were periodically reminded of how fortunate they were to have the services of Bette Davis—usually by Miss Davis herself, and with a lawsuit. She was right, though, because she brought them profits and prestige no other Warner's star could. William Wyler's 1938 **Jezebel** was her studio's answer to all the hubbub generated by David Selznick's pre-production hype on **Gone With The Wind**. Henry Fonda co-starred in this story of a headstrong Southern belle.

Facing page: A production still shows Bette Davis concentrating on the performance that would win her a second Academy Award. Standing next to her is the ubiquitous George Brent, and behind her are Henry O'Neill, Henry Fonda and Margaret Lindsay. **Jezebel** was photographed by Ernest Haller, Bette Davis' favorite cameraman; after losing the role of Scarlett O'Hara, Bette must have been equally galled to lose Ernie Haller for the extended period in which he worked on **Gone With The Wind**.

Pages 76–77: George Hurrell photographed Bette Davis for an ad campaign that said: 'Study this face!' The film being huckstered was Edmund Goulding's **Dark Victory**, produced in 1939 at Warner Brothers. This double exposure was accomplished in the photographic lab rather than in the camera. Each face was on a separate negative, already fully retouched. The two negatives were then consecutively projected onto a third negative in order to produce this composite image.

    The ivory-white texture of Bette Davis' face was achieved by deliberately bringing a spotlight closer to her face than the latitude of the film would accept, and in essence over-exposing it. The original negatives were then underdeveloped in order to restore some of the highlight detail.

    Bette Davis has often acknowledged her debt to Hurrell and others for advancing her career with images like these, but no one expected that their wizardry would one day be esteemed as fine art, fetching astronomical prices at chic galleries.

Above: When German impresario Max Reinhardt staged an impressive production of William Shakespeare's **A Midsummer Night's Dream** at the Hollywood Bowl, Warner Brothers decided to chance its transition to the screen. The result, co-directed by Warner's contract director William Dieterle, was a box-office failure whose losses were absorbed by the profits of wise-cracking films starring Bette Davis, James Cagney and Dick Powell. **A Midsummer Night's Dream** did, however, win an Academy Award for its sublime black-and-white photography, which was the work of Hal Mohr. Rarely have soft focus filters and shimmering backlighting been used as expressively and as cleverly.

Facing page: This still of Anita Louise as Titania by Bert Longworth gives only a hint of the overwhelming beauty of **A Midsummer Night's Dream**.

The executives at RKO Pictures were also interested in prestige pictures. They hoped that the overnight success of Katharine Hepburn in **A Bill of Divorcement** and **Morning Glory** would continue, giving them a profitable one-woman combination of Crawford and Garbo. Unfortunately for them, the Hepburn production team chose roles that neither of MGM's formidable ladies would have touched, and alienated the public and press as well.

Above: In George Cukor's 1935 **Sylvia Scarlet**, Katharine Hepburn spent most of the film disguised as a boy, disturbing both the other characters in the film and the few fans who saw it.

Above: Howard Hawks' 1938 **Bringing Up Baby** has become a bona fide classic if ever there was one, but at the time of its release, it served to cut both Hawks and Hepburn loose from RKO; it lost $365,000! This portrait shows Katharine Hepburn in a Howard Greer costume for **Bringing Up Baby**. It is also a good example of an Ernest Bachrach portrait. His trademark was the use of baby oil instead of makeup, then a soft spotlight and strong edgelights to create highlights on the skin's surface. Combined with glistening backgrounds, these highlights gave his subjects a burnished look, and gave his portraits an immediately recognizable tone. Of course, these techniques were borrowed from the innovative George Hurrell, but by the time Bachrach had perfected them, Hurrell had moved on to newer discoveries.

Above: Charles Boyer came to RKO for Phillip Moeller's 1935 **Break of Hearts**, another Hepburn failure, during which he sat for this portrait by Bachrach.

Facing page: Fred Astaire and Ginger Rogers were RKO's premiere moneymakers. They are shown here in a still from Mark Sandrich's 1937 **Shall We Dance**.

Above: Ronald Colman, here shown with Rosalind Russell, starred in Frank Lloyd's handsome production of Ouida's **Under Two Flags**, produced in 1936 at 20th Century-Fox. At this point in her career, Rosalind Russell was playing glamorous second leads, her comic talents as yet undiscovered.

Facing page: Humphrey Bogart spent the 1930s as a character actor, wasted in mostly inferior films because Warner Brothers executives failed to see the potential for stardom evident in portraits like this one from 1937.

Above: Gary Cooper and Lili Damita appeared in David Burton's **Fighting Caravans**, produced in 1931 at Paramount, a Western that was so well-produced that it required the talents of cameraman Lee Garmes.

Facing page: In this era, each major studio averaged two 'A' Westerns per year, but the smaller studios subsisted almost exclusively on receipts from the Saturday matinees. Even a middling studio like Columbia relied on low-budget Westerns, and John Wayne was their star. He is shown here in a 1932 Columbia Pictures portrait.

Romantic adventure films set in the nineteenth century became a staple of mid-Thirties filmmaking, partly due to the 1934 inception of the Legion of Decency: these films, based on Victorian literature, were exempted from the censor's toll.

Above: Henry King's 1936 **Ramona** helped Darryl F Zanuck's newly-merged 20th Century-Fox to continue growing. It featured lush Southern California scenery and Technicolor photography. In its first few years, Technicolor was a novelty more sought out by fledgling companies like 20th Century and Selznick than by companies like Metro, who didn't need audience lures. This scene still shows Kent Taylor and in the title role, the perennially popular Loretta Young.

Facing page: Before the merger, Darryl Zanuck's Twentieth Century Pictures borrowed Clark Gable from MGM for William Wellman's 1935 **Call of The Wild**.

Above: This in-character portrait of Harpo, Groucho and Chico Marx, circa 1935, by Ted Allan, shows their characteristic lunacy.

Facing page: This unretouched portrait of WC Fields came from the estate of Paramount still man Remy Morrison. It was shot against a white flat during the filming of **The Man on the Flying Trapeze**, a 1935 Clyde Bruckman production. The portrait was rejected by the publicity department for technical reasons, but Morrison had a confederate in the lab who made him a souvenir print.

Page 92: Myrna Loy was another player at MGM whose comic debut was long delayed. It finally took place in WS Van Dyke's 1934 **The Thin Man** and simultaneously gave birth to a long-lived series which co-starred William Powell and a dog called Asta. (On-set portrait by Ted Allan.)

Page 93: Cary Grant's rise to stardom was swift, thanks to a push from Mae West and Paramount's difficulties with Gary Cooper, to whom Grant was seen as a threat. This portrait dates from the mid-Thirties, when Grant's popularity was approaching Cooper's.

Above: MGM's musicals set industry standards by the late 1930s. Here are Nelson Eddy and Jeanette MacDonald in a dream setting designed by Cedric Gibbons and lit by Oliver Marsh for Robert Z Leonard's 1937 **Maytime**, one of the most profitable musicals of all time.

Facing page: Una Merkel comforts Evelyn Laye after the harsh rebuke of a ballet master in Dudley Murphy's **The Night Is Young**, produced in 1935 at MGM. This scene still is a good representation of cameraman James Wong Howe's Degas-inspired work.

More sequels were in order after the success of **The Bride Of Frankenstein**, and the studio came up with a literate script and a seasoned cast for 1936's **Dracula's Daughter**. Unfortunately, Lambert Hillyer was no James Whale, and the result was uneven, except for an occasionally inspired moment like this one, which is actually the work of an uncredited still man. Shown *(above)* are Nan Grey as the victim, and Gloria Holden, who gave an excellent performance as the vampire.

Facing page: **Rain**, John Colton's fine co-adaptation of Somerset Maugham's *Miss Sadie Thompson*, was filmed by Lewis Milestone for United Artists on Catalina Island in 1932. It starred Joan Crawford, who found the experience one of the most trying of her life. For her pains, she received the scorn of critics and the wrath of her fans—mostly for her slatternly makeup.
   The passage of 50 years has revealed that she was actually bearing the burden of an impossibly stagey group of supporting players, as well as the consistently off-key direction of Milestone. Other than Joan, only cameraman Oliver Marsh gave a fine accounting of himself.
   Perhaps the videocassette release of the complete **Rain** will finally disperse the apocrypha that discounted Joan's searing performance.

Above: The Samuel Goldwyn Studios turned out a product known for craftsmanship and scarcity, as exemplified by 1937, when his four releases included John Ford's masterful **The Hurricane**. This production still shows Ford seated behind the camera as Bert Glennon lines up a shot of Dorothy Lamour.

Facing page: Samuel Goldwyn hired George Hurrell to glamorize Anna Sten, a Russian actress he'd imported to compete with Garbo and Dietrich. Portraits such as this one could not prepare audiences for the oddness of her diction, and her first film, Dorothy Arzner's 1934 **Nana**, was a cruel disappointment. Still, Hurrell and his behind-the-movie-camera counterpart, Gregg Toland, found in her a superb subject.

Above: Like Samuel Goldwyn, David O Selznick depended on the distribution of only a handful of films at a time when the major studios were averaging 40 releases per year. One of his lesser-known products was John Cromwell's sentimental (1939) **Made For Each Other**. It starred Carole Lombard and James Stewart, here shown in a photographic study by Ted Allan, whom Selznick had lured away from MGM, thus causing Allan to be blackballed by LB Mayer.

Facing page: David Selznick's lasting contribution to American culture was **Gone With The Wind**. It was and is such a well-publicized production that my favorite stills from it have already been seen elsewhere and often. More than 1000 photographs make up its 'key set,' the sequentially numbered set of stills accumulated in a binder or binders for publicity purposes. The stills which fascinate me are the portraits made of Vivien Leigh before the film went into its Herculean production, images that show the woman Selznick saw when he auditioned her for the most important role in screen history. I include them in the hope that they will show a new facet of Miss Leigh's appeal, one captured by Laszlo Willinger in early 1939.

Above: A Laszlo Willinger portrait of Vivien Leigh taken before production began.

Facing page: A Clarence Bull portrait of Clark Gable as Rhett Butler taken during the filming of **Gone With The Wind**.

Before he founded Selznick International Pictures in 1936, David O Selznick had been a producer at both MGM and Paramount, and had seen the magic worked at these two studios by Daniels, Hurrell, Bull and Garmes. It was no surprise, then, that he launched **Gone With The Wind** with Bull portraits and Garmes camerawork; and it was with the help of at least four MGM contract directors that he completed it. I have always felt that this film, considered to be the apex of 1930s filmcraft, was really the synthesis of two studio styles: MGM and Paramount.

MGM and Paramount were Hollywood's glamour factories. Each boasted a staff of artisans and technicians who were able to transform neophytes into stars, and to transform established stars into even more rarefied images of themselves.

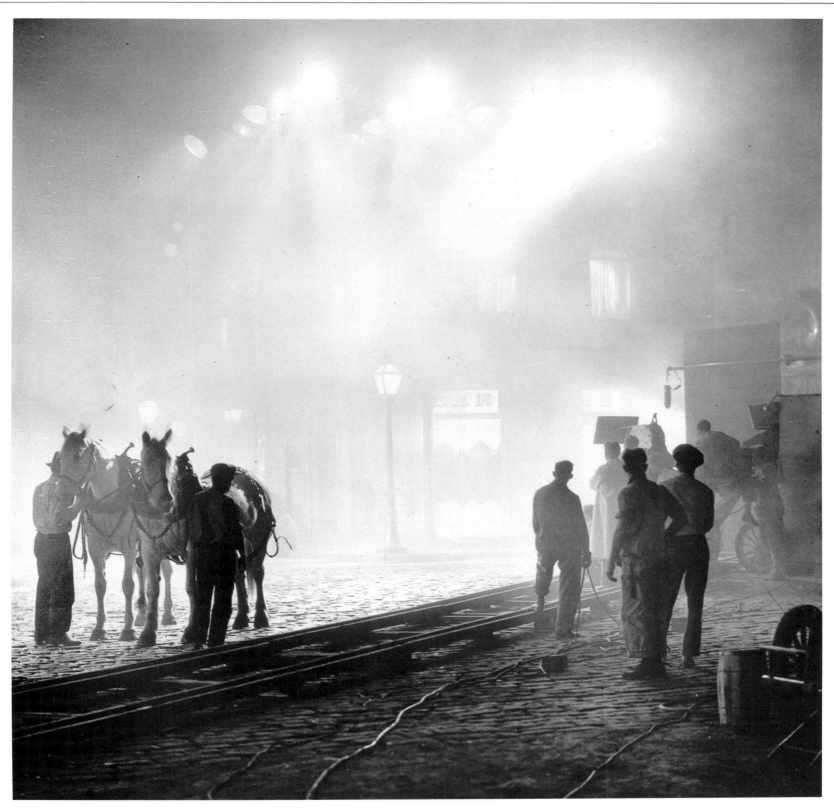

Facing page: As a movie still collector, I have consciously focused on glamour photography. It's natural, then, that the majority of the prints I've acquired were made at either Paramount or MGM. I enjoy tracing the discoveries and trends evident in the output of each studio, and making comparisons between the two studios' work. They were conscious rivals, but they influenced each other (as well as other studios), and they constantly borrowed from one another, too, as in the case of this seductive Willinger photograph of Vivien Leigh from **Gone With The Wind**.

Above: This production still from **Anna Christie** illustrates with what seriousness MGM regarded its arcana; they were abstracted and preserved for outsiders to marvel at.

Film historians have dubbed Paramount Pictures 'the continental studio' of the 1930s. Its films were crafted by emigre Europeans like Dreier, Sternberg and Lubitsch. They gave the typical Paramount film a texture and tone that was reminiscent of pre-World War I Vienna: lush, sentimental and slightly decadent. Paramount's best films were period films, and even if they took place in America's recent past, they had a gilded opulence that glowed like the inside of a memento-filled jewel box.

Above: Ernst Lubitsch's sophisticated comedies gave Paramount much of its luster and profit, and for a time he was head of production. He is seen here with Frances Drake and Henry Wilcoxon at a 1935 party honoring John E Otterson on the occasion of the latter's election to the presidency of Paramount.

Facing page: A typically Paramount image is this still shot of Fay Wray from Stephen Robert's nostalgic 1933 **One Sunday Afternoon**, which was photographed by Victor Milner and costumed by Travis Banton.

One reason for the Paramount 'glow' so often described by historians is the type of diffusion filter used by the camera department. In **Shanghai Express**, Lee Garmes experimented with different kinds of cloth filters to create soft focus effects, instead of using the customary glass diffusion disk. One gauze-like cloth, when dyed black and placed in front of the camera lens, created sparkling geometric patterns around highlights and softened the overall image. Sternberg took a liking to the effect and the cloth diffusion filter became a company standard.

Above: Paramount attempted to repeat the success of Marlene Dietrich with stage actress Tallulah Bankhead, but unfortunately did so without the help of worthwhile directors or scripts. The result was a series of pitifully bad films that drove the mannered Tallulah back to Broadway. Cloth-filtered stills like this one made me want to see Richard Wallace's **Thunder Below**, and when I finally did see it, I realized that the production still man had created a series of images much more interesting than anything in the film itself.

Facing page: Marlene Dietrich gets the cloth diffusion treatment in this costume test portrait for Josef von Sternberg's **The Scarlet Empress**. Note the highlights in her eyes.

Cecil B DeMille's name is inextricably linked with that of Paramount. **The Sign Of The Cross** saved the studio from bankruptcy in the throes of the Depression. The film captured the feeling of ancient Rome as few have been able to, thanks in part to cameraman Karl Struss's use of red cloth diffusion and Hans Dreier's imposing sets.

A production still from this 1932 epic shows *(left to right)* Elissa Landi as Mercia, the virtuous Christian girl; Frederic March as Marcus, the dissolute Roman officer; Karl Struss (in striped trousers); and Mr De-Mille himself. Behind DeMille's head is the aforementioned red cloth diffusion filter, into which a hole has been cut to create a 'soft edge

Top: Charles Laughton as Nero presides over the Circus Maximus, and at his right sits a young man whose pendant bears the inscription: *Neronis Servus*— ie, *Slave of Nero*.

DeMille, like Sternberg, allowed the still man on his productions as much time as necessary to capture the essence of each scene after it had been acted out for the movie camera.

Above: Christians leave the arena dungeon on their way to be martyred by lions, alligators and apes.

Top: Several of the most sensational scenes ever conceived by DeMille were cut from the negative of **The Sign of The Cross** when the film was re-released in 1944. They were considered too salacious and disturbing for wartime audiences. A 1981 audience at a DeMille centennial screening of the film in Los Angeles was treated to a complete print, and saw indeed how explicit was Ancaria's (Joyzelle Joyner's) *Dance of the Naked Moon*, which she performed to arouse Mercia at Marcus Superbus' orgy. If the scene hadn't been cut in 1944, it would certainly have been in 1948, when the film was sold to television. The complete **Sign Of The Cross** emerges as a wholly different film than the version currently available.

Above: Claudette Colbert's role as the villainous Poppaea made her a star, an affirmation of DeMille's practice of casting unknowns in his spectacles.

Mae West arrived in Hollywood on 16 June 1932, and within a year she was making movies as no one ever had. She was also doing what CB DeMille had done—saving Paramount from bankruptcy. Americans beleaguered by Depression worries were momentarily forgetting them, thanks to the original humor of this controversial actress-playwright. Her humour was too original for some people, notably the sanctimonious women's clubs, who complained volubly that censorship was needed.

Facing page: One minority reviewer wrote: 'There is no more pretense of romance here than on a stud farm.' Mae West made four films in this vein before the prudes overtook her. This uncredited portrait is from the second of them, the classic **She Done Him Wrong**, produced in 1933 at Paramount, which was directed by sometime-actor Lowell Sherman.

Above: Jean Harlow's career was also changed by censorship, and not for the better. This George Hurrell portrait was made less than a month after the Labor Day 1932 suicide of her husband, producer Paul Bern.

Above: Metro-Goldwyn-Mayer Pictures is my favorite studio, but its founding father, Louis B Mayer, is not my favorite Hollywood person, nor even among my favorites; but then *Nil nisi bonum de mortuis. . .** This 1934 portrait of LB was executed by Russell Ball.

Above: In my estimation, the brightest star at MGM was none other than Irving G Thalberg, who from 1924 to 1936 was the creative force responsible for the studio's finest achievements. This candid photo was taken of him and his wife Norma Shearer, with Louis B Mayer, at the Pasadena train station in 1933.

Facing page: The Thalbergs attended a Gay Nineties party in 1933, and the hostess, Carole Lombard, was thoughtful enough to have a photographer on hand to shoot pictures like this.

*'Of the dead, nothing but good should be spoken.'

Above: As a manager of MGM's still photo department, Clarence Bull initiated a practice unique to his company. He invented a device that imprinted the date, film production number, exposure number, and credit on the edge of an exposed negative before processing. That is how we know that this portrait of Greta Garbo was shot on 17 May 1935, charged to account #530 (general publicity), was shot by Clarence Bull and was exposure #129. This portrait was made for **Anna Karenina** publicity and is unusual in that Bull is using a soft focus lens, a practice that for all intents and purposes he abandoned in 1930—just after newcomer George Hurrell had created a sensation by shooting portraits with razor-sharp commercial lenses.

Above: Jeanette MacDonald was starring in Robert Z Leonard's **Broadway Serenade** when she posed for this 1939 Bull portrait.

Leo the Lion roared before every MGM movie, but Clarence Sinclair Bull put his personal stamp just as surely on every single photographic print that left the Culver City plant.

Above: Herbert Marshall was still a leading man when Clarence Bull made this portrait of him for Edmund Goulding's 1935 psychological drama **The Flame Within**.

Facing page: MGM borrowed Gary Cooper from Paramount for the Cosmopolitan production of Richard Boleslavsky's **Operator 13**. Clarence Bull made this portrait on 17 April 1934.

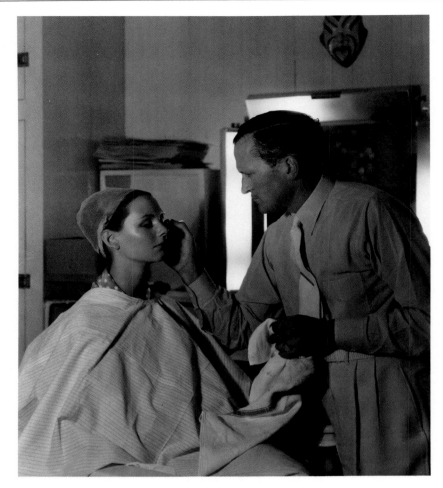

Above: Virgil Apger was an assistant to Clarence Bull in the portrait gallery before being set loose on the MGM lot to shoot assignments like this one, which shows makeup department head Jack Dawn applying finishing touches to Elizabeth Allan's makeup, which in actuality Elizabeth herself applied in her own dressing room!

Facing page: The finished product as she appeared on the set of George Cukor's endearing 1934 classic, **David Copperfield**. The costume worn by Miss Allan was designed not by Gilbert Adrian, but by Dolly Tree, who also began to design for Jean Harlow when she changed her image.

Above: Travis Banton was Paramount's talented couturier. His work for Cecil B DeMille's 1934 **Cleopatra** still shows up at museum exhibitions as an example of imaginative, finely detailed costume design.

Facing page: Although Claudette Colbert was suffering from flu during much of her work on **Cleopatra**, her performance never did. This scene still shows her riding a slave-borne litter into Rome.

'Gowns by Adrian' in the credits of an MGM movie meant that there would be at least one entrance worthy of gasps. Not all the dresses he designed would become as famous as Harlow's **Dinner At Eight** dress, but they certainly amplified the characterization of any actress who was wearing them.

Examples include Billie Burke and Marie Dressler *(facing page)* in **Dinner at Eight** ; and Greta Garbo *(above)* in **Queen Christina**.

Above left: Still man Milton Brown shot this on-set portrait of Jeanette MacDonald in Ernst Lubitsch's **The Merry Widow**. This 1934 film was an example of the cross-fertilization which took place between MGM and Paramount. MacDonald and Chevalier had made a series of successful musicals at Paramount, some with Lubitsch. Irving Thalberg picked up MacDonald after Paramount dropped her, and then sought to re-form the original trio by borrowing Chevalier and Lubitsch from Paramount. The result was a gorgeous hybrid: the film looked like a Paramount film, sounded like an MGM musical, and cost more than two of their films combined. It didn't recoup that cost, either.

Above right: Jeanette MacDonald in The **Firefly**—'gown by Adrian'. Also coutured by Gilbert Adrian's deft hand, Talullah Bankhead is seen in this still *(facing page)* from **Faithless**, gazing at a portrait which you will see on *page 133*.

George Hurrell stands unchallenged as the greatest of all Hollywood portrait photographers. By the time I started collecting movie stills, original prints of his work were already as scarce as hen's teeth. Eventually though, I did manage to acquire a representative sampling of his work, the best of which I include in this text. The 1981 portrait of Mr Hurrell *(above)* was taken in connection with a gallery exhibition of his work. The photographer was Jeff Goldwater.

Compare his portrait of Jeanette MacDonald *(facing page)* to that on *page 128* and you will understand why Hurrell is considered the greatest. His genius lay in not only seeing his subjects differently, but in innovative techniques that transferred that vision to the film in entirely new ways. Jeanette never looked better. Lillian Bond *(below)* was a supporting player, but George Hurrell lavished the same glamour treatment on her that he did on established stars, giving her a timeless allure.

Above: Wallace Beery in a 1930 portrait by George Hurrell for George Hill's classic **Min and Bill**.

Facing page: Hurrell's innovation of the boom light for more dramatic backlighting can be seen in this 1931 portrait of Robert Montgomery for **The Easiest Way**, a Jack Conway production.

Facing page: Mae West's rendition of *I Wonder Where My Easy Rider's Gone* was one of the many high points in Lowell Sherman's **She Done Him Wrong**. Mae's costume was created by novice designer Edith Head.

Above: This production still shows Mae rehearsing her song. She was well-photographed in this, her second film. Charles Lang made sure that she looked younger than her 45-odd years.

Paramount lost only prestige to MGM by loaning Lubitsch and Chevalier: Mae West, meanwhile, was breaking box office records with **She Done Him Wrong**.

Above, left: 'Get Bill Daniels!' was the injunction whispered to Ethel Barrymore by brother John when she arrived in Hollywood to join him and Lionel for MGM's **Rasputin And The Empress**.

Above, right: Since Garbo was away in Sweden, and Norma Shearer was now using Lee Garmes, Ethel did indeed get Bill Daniels, who lit her to good effect.

Above: Still man Milton Brown lit Lionel Barrymore to scary effect in this off-set portrait. *Below:* This is how Milton Brown made the portrait above, using an Agfa-Ansco 8x10 view camera, a double broad (pictured) and a baby spot (not pictured).

Facing page: This scene still shows the Barrymore siblings in their only film together, Richard Boleslavsky's **Rasputin and The Empress**, produced in 1932 at MGM. The Czar was portrayed by Ralph Morgan—and his hemophiliac son, by Tad Alexander.

China Seas, directed by Tay Garnett from a fine script by Jules Furthman, was released in mid-1935. It was the end of an era for Jean Harlow *(above)*. Never again would she wear an Adrian gown or platinum blonde hair. Fortunately, this film was a fitting swan song to her brassy persona; it was robust, risqué and glamorous. Clark Gable *(below)* endured a horrific torture scene in **China Seas**.

Facing page: Harlow was ideal for Hurrell and vice versa—as shown by this spring 1935 portrait, in which Jean wore a hair style from the just-completed **Reckless** and a gown from her next film, **China Seas**.

Facing page: This strange ethereal study was made in 1934, when Hurrell was doing a Harlow sitting for **The Girl from Missouri**.

Above: Jean Harlow in the spring of 1937. History has overlooked this winsome ash-blonde image in favor of the platinum bombshell of films like **Dinner at Eight**. This was Harlow's last sitting with George Hurrell. She died less than two months later, under circumstances so mysterious that they may never be truly explained.

It is my contention that the entire issue of Hollywood glamour in the 1930s can be divided into two schools: Paramount and MGM. Paramount, as has been shown, had a golden continental glow. MGM strove for a sophisticated American gloss. If a rivalry existed between them, it was because the most touted product of each studio centered on a glamorous European woman, and fans could not be expected to enjoy both: the Dietrich fans and the Garbomaniacs had their separate camps and the studios catered to them.

Also hoping for defection, the studios saw to it that the careers of those two actresses ran on parallel tracks all through the 1930s. In the 1931 **Dishonored**, Dietrich's second American film, she played a Great War spy. Eight months later, Garbo was **Mata Hari**. Dietrich's **Blonde Venus** explored milieus identical to **Susan Lenox**, **Shanghai Express** followed **Grand Hotel**, and even comic forays like **Destry Rides Again** and **Ninotchka** were simultaneously released. This correspondence would have been pointless had these stars not been such thoroughly individual entities.

Above: The deliberately inscrutable Josef von Sternberg, here in a Laszlo Willinger portrait, used portrait sittings to define and perfect Marlene Dietrich's successive images.

Above: This is how Marlene Dietrich first greeted the American public. Gene Richee made this 1930 portrait, and then Josef von Sternberg decided to take a more active part in the process.

Facing page: In less than two years, the creation had become as inscrutable as the creator, and Sternberg had made more discoveries about lighting than most photographers make in a lifetime.

Above: William Walling received nominal credit for this and other portraits of Dietrich, but Sternberg supervised their every aspect.

Facing page: Marlene Dietrich in male attire was at first shocking to the American public.

Above: Travis Banton's gowns played an important part in the iconization of Dietrich—as is shown by his use of black velvet and black net gloves in this 1933 portrait.

Facing page: Another important Dietrich prop was the cigarette, and its attendant plume of smoke—as carefully arranged as her hair, of course. This 1935 portrait reflects Sternberg's practice of making portraits between films in order to find new looks for his favorite subject.

In the 1930s, Garbo had no single mentor as Dietrich had in Sternberg. She did, however, have a single portrait photographer, but her arrangement with him and MGM was quite different from Dietrich's at Paramount. Garbo would only pose for portraits in connection with the one film she made per year—and then only on one day at production's end. Therefore, Clarence Bull was required to shoot all the portraits needed to publicize that film, including all changes of costume and hairstyle, in the course of a single day. He overcame this handicap to create the following images.

Above: This 1932 portrait sitting was sandwiched between the finish of **Grand Hotel** and the start of **As You Desire Me**, because Garbo wanted to rush off to Sweden after the completion of the latter. As a result, she wore the hairstyles of the former with the gowns of the latter, thoroughly confusing fans and fan magazines.

Facing page: This portrait for **Queen Christina** was made on 26 October 1933.

Clarence Bull stated that Garbo inspired him as did no other subject. It's true that he tried effects during her sittings that appear nowhere else in his work. Bull did not feel compelled to throw long eyelash shadows, but he did enjoy photographing Garbo with her eyes closed, as in this portrait *(below),* made for George Cukor's **Camille**. A similar effect, but a different mood, was captured by Bull *(above)* for Clarence Brown's **Conquest**.

Facing page: Garbo had been ill during the making of **Camille**—troubled by Bill Daniels' alcoholic woes, and saddened by Irving Thalberg's untimely death. This portrait reflects some of the real-life tragedy that became part of her portrayal.

Above: Clarence Bull took pride in his achievement of lighting a portrait solely by candlelight.

Facing page: Bull showed Garbo at her most sublime in this 1939 portrait for Ernst Lubitsch's **Ninotchka**.

Above: Joe and Marlene together in 1933. The last film of the Sternberg-Dietrich alliance was 1935's **The Devil is A Woman**, and it surpassed their previous efforts in its complexity of design and theme. Some historians say that the plot of **The Devil is A Woman** was a thinly disguised retelling of a sado-masochistic affair between the director and his discovery. As evidence, they point to the strong resemblence between Lionel Atwill *(below, left* with Marlene), the film's main charac-ter, and Sternberg himself. When asked about this, Sternberg replied with his usual opacity: 'In my films, everyone is me.'

Facing page: Travis Banton outdid himself, not to mention the needle-women who labored for weeks to complete this white lace dress for **The Devil is A Woman**.

Above: Bill Daniels was for 15 years Garbo's cameraman. He is seen here conferring with her on the first day of shooting on **Ninotchka**. It was their last film together.

Below: Many moments in Daniels' films, like this one from **Anna Karenina**, exist simply to pay homage to Garbo's beauty. Her directors knew this and allowed Daniels that liberty. MGM occasionally made frame enlargements from the editor's work print if the still man for some reason had not captured a particularly noteworthy setup. I found this print in a dusty antique store in Glendale.

Facing page: This scene still by William Grimes shows a Daniels-lit moment from George Cukor's **Camille**, produced in 1937 at MGM.

Above: Unlike Sternberg, Bill Daniels could use outdoor lighting as effectively as indoor stage effects; as in this scene from **Camille**, with Garbo and Robert Taylor.

Facing page: When it came to indoor lighting effects, though, there was no one more clever than Bill Daniels. His clever use of 'practicals'—ie, stage lamps concealed in what would appear to be actual sources of light — gave all of his films a three-dimensional look. This scene still is from Rouben Mamoulian's **Queen Christina**.

Below: Film editor Chester W Schaeffer began his career in the summer of 1930 as an assistant to Hugh Wynn on the German language version of **Anna Christie**. He regaled me with many a story, including his recollection of sitting next to Garbo in the projection room as she watched the rushes to check her accent and pronunciation. 'She laughed out loud at herself—very deep! A guffaw, almost. I never forgot it. I wish now that I'd saved some of those outtakes. Think what they'd be worth. . . '

Above, both: Greta Garbo as she appeared in her first scene in the German **Anna Christie**. Chet Schaeffer told me that foreign-language dubbing was at this time unknown, as well as subtitles, so the only way to tap the highly profitable European market for early talkies was to do several versions of the same film. The American version had premiered in March, and then French director Jacques Feyder had been engaged to direct this version. It went more quickly than the first, for which two different Garbo entrances had been shot.

Facing page: An enigmatic scene from **Mata Hari** excised by the censor's hand.

This beautiful scene from Richard Boleslavsky's **The Painted Veil** never appeared on the screen. The first three scenes were scrapped and re-shot, for reasons that Chester Schaeffer could not remember. Garbo is shown here with Herbert Marshall in a Milton Brown still of a Bill Daniels scene in a Cedric Gibbons setting.

Hal Rosson replaced Bill Daniels on **Camille** *(facing page, top)* when Daniels disappeared for three days (Karl Freund finished the picture). Garbo *(facing page bottom* in **Ninotchka**) always knew her lines letter-perfect, so she would wait on the edge of the set while other actors rehearsed. *Above:* This shot was taken from the catwalks by William Grimes and shows Garbo rehearsing the mazurka with Phoebe Foster as Clarence Brown points to her—on the set of **Anna Karenina**.

Above: Ramon Novarro and Myrna Loy emote in a Cedric Gibbons setting for Sam Wood's 1933 **The Barbarian**, with lighting by Hal Rosson.

Facing page, top: Much of the gloss that was MGM can be attributed to Cedric Gibbons *(below)*, head of the art department, and although he did not personally design every film's sets, he dictated the gleaming style that unified the Metro 'look.'

Facing page, below: George Fitzmaurice's 1932 **Mata Hari**, just before the censor eliminated Novarro and Garbo's next scene, which took place beyond the satin curtains.

Edmund Goulding *(above)* was the consummate English gentleman and a sought-after 'actor's director.' His **Grand Hotel** remains a classic after half a century because of the subtleties of playing he got from his all-star cast. In the Milton Brown behind-the-scenes still *(below)*, Goulding takes a much-needed break from directing Greta Garbo's famous 'I want to be alone' scene.

Facing page: This publicity department composite highlights the stellar cast of **Grand Hotel**: Lionel Barrymore, Lewis Stone, Jean Hersholt, Wallace Beery, John Barrymore, Joan Crawford and Greta Garbo. Contrary to what you may have read, Garbo did not pose for a group shot on the set; composites like this were the only way to show the entire cast.

The most intense rivalry in Hollywood was not between Paramount and Metro or between Dietrich and Garbo. It existed within the walls of MGM, and had since 1925, when Joan Crawford got her first movie job—as a double for Norma Shearer. From then on, Joan envied Norma's ever-ascending status as she envied no other, even though her own following was large and vocal. She resented Norma Shearer's position as First Lady of MGM and the fact that Norma had first choice of scripts, directors and cameramen. This frustrating situation continued until the 1936 death of Norma's husband Irving Thalberg, who was, incidentally, vice-president of Metro.

Joan's lot did not improve substantially after this, but she did have the opportunity to vent her fury at Norma in several legendary confrontations, most of which stemmed from Norma's attempts to summarily deprive her of the services of Bill Daniels or Laszlo Willinger. Joan was a fighter, and she'd fought for every inch of her progress at MGM, just as fiercely as she fought her way up the social ladder in her movies. Perhaps that is why her name comes to mind whenever the word 'star' is mentioned.

Norma Shearer was no less a star of the 1930s, but what she and Joan did not consciously realize was that each balanced the other's image at the studio, much as Garbo and Dietrich complemented one another from across town. Joan and Norma were unique, too, but their respective insecurities could not admit the possibility of peaceful co-existence.

This invidious relationship lasted through the glory years at MGM and accounted for some of the best work done there. If Joan and Norma brought out the best in their artists, too, it was because each star demanded the same of herself, usually stopping just short of exhaustion.

Facing page: This is the effect of Oliver Marsh's lighting: enough key light to define the bone structure and shape of her face, and yet a glowing luminosity in the shadow areas. Note how Joan's eyes glisten in this scene still from Clarence Brown's 1934 **Sadie McKee**.

Above: Clark Gable and Norma Shearer in Clarence Brown's 1931 **A Free Soul**, the sort of sophisticated vehicle in which she excelled.

Right: Bill Daniels assumed the role of Norma Shearer's personal cameraman when Lee Garmes moved to Europe and Ray June proved unworthy on **Riptide**. Bill's lighting was flattering because it was precise, taking into account the age lines under Norma's neck and the lines under her eyes, which he hid by dimming one light and bringing up another whenever she turned her head.

He also knew to watch for her legendary eye problem; the muscle of her left eye did not pull sufficiently to align it to her right eye whenever she looked out and over to the left, causing her to appear cross-eyed. It was this problem that necessitated 28 takes on the set of **Marie Antoinette**, an almost unendurable embarrassment for director WS Van Dyke—who was better known as 'One-Take Woody.'

Facing page: Norma Shearer in a Daniels-lit setting from George Cukor's **Romeo and Juliet** (1936). If Bill didn't make Norma look 14, he certainly made her look younger than her full 35 years. He also made this film a rich tapestry of light and shadow that remains unseen and unappreciated by historians or audiences.

Above: Joan Crawford's allies included this man, the aforementioned Woody Van Dyke, who directed more hit films than all the rest of MGM's contract directors combined. He was valuable to Joan because he helped her to poke gentle fun at her self-consciously glamorous image, in films like **Love On The Run**.

Facing page, bottom: Cameraman George Folsey told me how he spent hours glamorizing Joan with carefully placed spots and scrims and cutters, only to have her delay the filming of the scene by insisting that he walk around the set with her, arm in arm, as she let her eyes brim with tears, preparing herself for the scene and embarrassing him to death.

Facing page, top: An example of the Van Dyke-Folsey-Crawford collaboration. This scene from **Forsaking All Others** (1934) was obviously designed for black-and-white photography.

Above: Still man Frankie Tanner was another of Joan's favorites. He took this candid of her as she awaited a cue on the set of Dorothy Arzner's 1937 **The Bride Wore Red**. This film had been begun by the articulate director Richard Boleslavsky, but he died partway into the production—not of poisoned water, as has been erroneously written, but of a heart attack on the golf course.

Facing page: Oliver Marsh's lighting and the Crawford intensity elevate this Frank Tanner still to the level of portraiture. It was shot for Howard Hawks' 1933 **Today We Live**.

Facing page: Norma Shearer's greatest contribution to film history may have been her campaign to have George Hurrell hired by MGM. Hurrell worked there from 1929 to 1933, quit, and then opened his own studio on the Sunset Strip, where he shot this 1934 portrait of Norma Shearer for Edmund Goulding's **Riptide**.

Above: For once, Joan benefited from one of Norma's career advancements. Hurrell's portraits did more for her than for any star of the period, including Norma. Joan could not know it at the time, but Hurrell's images of her have underwritten her immortality.

Above: Norma's patrician profile was the delight of every photographer who worked with her. This portrait was made for Sidney Franklin's 1932 **Smilin' Through**.

Above: 1934's **The Barretts of Wimpole Street** occasioned this Hurrell portrait. Sidney Franklin's direction gave Norma one of her best showcases.

Above: This transcendent portrait of Norma was one of the last Hurrell made of her; it dates from later 1935, and was shot in connection with a fitting by designer Irene.

Above: Another 1934 Hurrell portrait; I once asked him how he compensated for the smallness of Norma's eyes. 'I had her look up,' he answered offhandedly.

Above: This smoldering Joan Crawford portrait was made for Nick Grinde's 1931 **This Modern Age**.

Facing page: Hurrell painted word-pictures in the minds of his subjects when he talked to them during sittings; Joan found this technique helpful in evoking the kind of mood shown in this portrait, in which she wore a costume from the 1934 **Forsaking All Others**. If the costume is not recognizable—Hurrell had Joan partially remove it, the better to expose her famous shoulders.

Above: Joan Crawford and Norma Shearer co-starred in the 1939 George Cukor classic **The Women**. By the end of production, when Laszlo Willinger made this portrait, the two stars were not speaking, save through agents and vituperative telegrams. The 15-year-old rivalry had erupted into a feud, rendered pointless because the ground they were fighting over was already slipping from beneath their feet; 1940 was just around the corner, and with it would come the Twilight of the Goddesses. . .

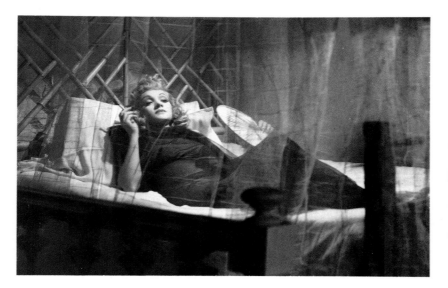

Above: Marlene Dietrich used her knowledge of staging and lighting and went on to conquer new screens and new stages.

Facing page: Garbo made an indecisive exit, then deciding that the magic aura of the 1930s was gone, decided not to come back.

'We are no other than a moving row. . .

. . .Of Magic Shadow-shapes that come and go. . .

. . .Round with the Sun-illumin'd Lantern held. . .

'. . .In Midnight by the Master of the Show.'

Index

Alexander, Tad: 22
Allan, Elizabeth: 122, 123
Astaire, Fred: 69, 83
Atwill, Lionel: 154

Bankhead, Tallulah: 108, 126
Barrymore, Ethel: 37, 136, 137
Barrymore, John: 36, 136, 137, 169
Barrymore, Lionel: 136, 137, 169
Beery, Wallace: 132
Bennett, Constance: 53
Bogart, Humphrey: 85
Bond, Lillian: 130
Bow, Clara: 11, 20
Boyer, Charles: 82
Brent, George: 75
Brisson, Carl: 58, 59
Brown, Clarence: 10, 165
Brown, Milton: 136
Bull, Clarence: 40
Burke, Billie: 129
Burke, Kathleen: 62

Cabot, Bruce: 51
Cagney, James: 70
Carlisle, Kitty: 58, 59
Colbert, Claudette: 32, 113, 125
Colman, Ronald: 84
Cooper, Gary: 15, 62–63, 86, 121, 189
Crawford, Joan: 39, 97, 169, 171, 175–177, 181, 182, 183, 184, 189
Cromwell, Richard: 62

Damita, Lili: 86
Daniels, William: 22, 172
Davies, Marion: 57
Davis, Bette: 74, 75, 76–77
Dawn, Jack: 122
Del Rio, Dolores: 73
DeMille, Cecil B: 110–111
Denny, Reginald: 12
DeHavilland, Olivia: 72
Dietrich, Marlene: 17, 18–19, 21, 24, 64, 65, 109, 142–147, 154, 155, 184
Dione, Rose: 46–47
Dressler, Marie: 14
Dumbrille, Douglas: 62

Eddy, Nelson: 94

Fields, W C: 90
Fleming, Victor: 52
Flynn, Errol: 72
Folsey, George: 175
Fonda, Henry: 74, 75
Ford, John: 98
Foster, Phoebe: 165

Gable, Clark: 23, 32, 89, 102, 138, 172
Garbo, Greta: 10, 25, 42, 43, 44–45, 118, 127, 148–153, 158–159, 160, 161, 162–163, 165, 167, 169, 185, 188, 192
Garmes, Lee: 22
George, Gladys: 70
Gibbons, Cedric: 166
Gilbert, John: 13
Glennon, Bert: 98
Goulding, Edmund: 168, 170
Grant, Cary: 93
Grey, Nan: 96

Harlow, Jean: 1, 35, 52, 115, 138–141
Hayes, Helen: 63
Hepburn, Katharine: 80–81
Hersholt, Jean: 169
Holden, Gloria: 96
Hopkins, Miriam: 68
Hurrell, George: 130

Johnson, Kay: 12
Joyner, Joyzelle: 113

Karloff, Boris: 26, 48
Keith, Ian: 43, 44–45, 46–47

Lamour, Dorothy: 98
Lanchester, Elsa: 27, 28–29
Landi, Elissa: 33, 110–111
Laughton, Charles: 26–27, 112
Laye, Evelyn: 95
Leigh, Vivien: 101, 103, 104
Lindsay, Margaret: 75
Lombard, Carole: 54, 55, 60–61, 100
Louise, Anita: 79
Loy, Myrna: 40, 48, 92, 166
Lubitsch, Ernst: 106
Lugosi, Bela: 48

MacDonald, Jeanette: 8–9, 94, 119, 128, 131
Mackaill, Dorothy: 18–19

March, Frederic: 71, 110–111
Marshall, Herbert: 120, 162–163, 170
Marx Brothers, The: 91
Mayer, Louis B: 116
Merkel, Una: 95
Michael, Gertrude: 56
Montgomery, Robert: 133
Muni, Paul: 49

Novarro, Ramon: 8–9, 167

Oakie, Jack: 59
O'Day, Nell: 30
O'Neill, Henry: 75

Powell, William: 92

Raft, George: 60–61
Rogers, Ginger: 34, 69, 83
Rosson, Harold: 164
Russell, Rosalind: 84

Schaeffer, Chester W: 160
Shearer, Norma: 7, 22, 23, 116, 117, 170, 172, 173, 180–181, 184
Starrett, Charles: 48
Sten, Anna: 99
Sternberg, Josef von: 16, 142, 154
Stewart, James: 100
Stone, Lewis: 169
Stuart, Gloria: 31
Struss, Karl: 110–111

Taylor, Kent: 88
Thalberg, Irving G: 116, 117
Tone, Franchot: 62
Truex, Ernest: 33

Van Dyke, Woodbridge Strong: 174

Wayne, John: 87
Weissmuller, Johnny: 41
Welles, Orson: 190
West, Mae: 114, 134–135
Wong, Anna May: 66–67
Wray, Fay: 51, 107
Wynyard, Diana: 38

Young, Loretta: 88

Pages 186–187: A Milton Brown still from William K Howard's **Vanessa: Her Love Story** (1934 – MGM). *Page 188:* A Clarence Bull portrait of Garbo for **Anna Karenina**. *Page 189:* A Frank Tanner still of Gary Cooper and Joan Crawford on the set of **Today We Live**. *Facing page:* An uncredited portrait of Orson Welles in his **Citizen Kane**, produced in 1941 at RKO. *Page 192:* An 'eclipse lighting' portrait of Garbo by Bull, 1939.